Foraging

A Guide to discovering delicious, edible
wild plants, and fungi.

Charlie Hughes

—

Contents

—

Introduction

I want to thank you and for buying the book, "Foraging: A Guide to discovering delicious, edible wild plants, and fungi.

This book contains information on how to take advantage of the abundance of free food provided by Mother Nature. It includes information on:-

What sort of foods you can forage and where to go to forage them.

- How you can find and identify different species of fungi.

- What plants, flowers, nuts and fruits are safe for you to consume.

- Tips on sustaining the food source while enjoying all it has to offer.

- How you can store your wild food so you can enjoy it all year round.

Foraging is a fun way to bring down your weekly shopping bills and enjoy the outdoors. So what are you waiting for, turn the pages and learn how to re-acquaint yourself with Mother Nature.

Thanks again for buying this book, I hope you enjoy it!

Chapter 1 – What Is Foraging?

Foraging is the act of sourcing and gathering edible foods from nature. For centuries people the world over have looked to nature to provide them with the resources needed to maintain a healthy heart and mind.

As recent as World War Two, foraging was a popular and accepted element of the British culture, but with the introduction and promotion of convenience foods, foraging became an outdated, and mostly forgotten, skill.

In recent years the popularity of pre-packaged and processed foods has waned and we are once again turning our minds towards the gathering of wild food sources. Every year, more and more people are using allotments, turning their flower beds into vegetable gardens and venturing out into the country lanes and woodland area's to seek out edible wild foods supplied by Mother Nature herself.

No matter where you live, whether you are surrounded by miles of countryside or deep in the heart of a bustling city, once you know what to look for you will find a treasure trove of delicious, nutritious and free food just waiting to be foraged.

In many parts of Eastern Europe, foraging is still a regular activity. Solitary foraging can be fun and is normal practice but many people gather a group of family and friends and incorporate foraging into a fun day out.

However you choose to do it, it is a great way to relax and connect with the nature around you. And foraging does not just provide sustenance; it is excellent for your mood too. The feeling of returning home and preparing a mouth watering meal or snack, using food that you have foraged yourself, is extremely satisfying.

You will be re-connecting with that primal part of you that the convenience of modern day living has suppressed.

There is no limitation on when and where edible foraged foods can be found, from dark forests to open fields, your own back garden or even in-between the cracks in the pavement just outside your front door, nature will always have something to offer.

What is available for foraging changes from season to season so there will always be something different around to tempt your taste-buds.

Chapter 2 – Foraging Guidelines

As with any activity, there are do's and don'ts involved in foraging your own food. Some are there for health reasons, some are environmental and others are simple common sense. Regardless of the reason, they should all be followed when venturing out to collect wild food.

Introducing foraged food into your diet

Natural wild foods are often stronger and fuller flavored than the regular supermarket foods which your body and palate is used to. Introduce foraged foods into your diet in small quantities to give your digestive system and taste buds time to adjust to it.

As with any food source, too much of something your body is not used to, can result in an upset stomach, so take it slowly.

There is also a minor risk of having an allergic reaction so introducing it in increments can save you from a severe adverse physical reaction. With anything new to you, start by rubbing a small amount onto your forearm. If, after a couple of hours, your body has not reacted to it then go ahead and eat a small amount. If there is still no reaction and you have established that your body is happy to accept the food being offered, then you can really 'Go Wild' with your meals.

Identification of Wild Food

Do not attempt to learn everything all in one go. There is a huge variety of wild nuts, berries, plants, flowers and fungi out there and many of them bear striking similarities to others. It is extremely easy to mistake one food source for another. Easy and potentially fatal!

Disclaimer: *Always be certain to check that you have correctly identified anything you eat as being safe before attempting to consume it.*

Poisoning from misidentification of foraged foods is responsible for many hospital admissions each year, so learning to identify exactly what you are foraging is essential.

Start with learning to identify just a few items to forage, it would be useful to have a picture of some sort with you, (or an expert), to start with to make sure you are sure about what you are collecting. Learn to recognize them by sight and smell and know the similarities they may have to other foods.

As you become confident about the knowledge you have then you can start to add a few more items to identify. Before long you will have a list of food sources that you can recognize instantly.

I will put as much descriptive information as I can in the food list but always make sure you are aware of what you are eating.

Sustainability

Strange as it may seem, there are many varieties of wild food which are becoming so rare that they are now protected. As foraging rises in popularity, the risk that many varieties of plant and fungi will become endangered continues to grow.

There are two simple rules which you can easily apply to your foraging habits that will help to reduce the risk of this.

- The first requires nothing more than keeping your eyes open to what is around you. If you see something you would like to forage, take a look around and notice if there are more of the same in the local vicinity. If it is a solitary plant or species of fungi, leave it alone, if there are several more growing close by then forage it, but take only what you require.

- The second is nothing more than your foraging technique. Unless you are going to be using the root, always cut your plant, leaf or fungi cleanly above ground.

By ripping out the entire plant simply to gain a few leaves or a little piece of the fungi, you are damaging the roots and removing its seed which will prevent re-growth.

Similarly, if you do require the whole plant, (or even if you don't), scatter its seed around a little so more will grow.

Plant Environment

Pesticides, animal waste and pollutants can damage the flavor and quality of wild foods, so keep this in mind when planning, and during, your foraging exploits.

Try to take items from area's that are not in close proximity to industrial manufacturing plants or crop farms who regularly use spray pesticides and fertilizers.

Heavily trafficked roadsides are also best avoided unless you are foraging from at least 100 feet away from the curb side.

Wherever you forage from, always make certain that you have rinsed any food items before consuming them to remove any unwanted residue.

Familiarisation

Next time you walk your dog and take a stroll to the local shop, have a look around you. Learn what produce you can find for free in your local area.

How many trees do you have in your local park? What nuts and berries grow on them? Do you have fungi growing from the trunk and branches of any of those trees? What treats are hiding in the grass and under the bushes? Even the cracks in the walls sprout delicious ingredients that can turn a basic casserole or plain salad into a different meal.

Learn about your local environment and the food that grows there. Identify it and discover the other items that can commonly be found growing alongside or near to it.

Understanding the nature of the food you forage, rather than just the qualities inherent to it, will give you a much better insight into the influence of your food source on its surrounding environment and bring about a substantial difference in the amount of local food you can forage.

Chapter 3 – Storing Your Foraged Food

If possible it is always better to eat your foraged food while it is fresh, but as many wild foods are seasonal you may want to store some for the months when it isn't readily available.

Freezing Foraged Foods

While frozen foraged food is not suitable to eat raw once defrosted, they are perfectly edible once cooked and can greatly enhance a cooked meal.

Before freezing always rinse any foraged food items and shake of the excess water. The can then be frozen whole or chopped and frozen.

It is best to spread your food out on a tray when you freeze it to stop it from clumping together. Once frozen, it can then be put separated into useable portion sizes and frozen in an airtight container or sealable freezer bag.

Drying your Foraged Foods

Traditionally, foraged foods were dried to preserve them and there are several different methods which work for this purpose. Drying your food has the added benefit that it is easily accessible and has a long shelf life.

When stored correctly, dried wild food will remain a valuable addition to your recipes for one to two years. Always store in an airtight container, a jar, tub or re-sealable bag are all ideal for this purpose. You should also ensure that they are stored away from direct sunlight and kept away from moisture.

There are three ways to dry your wild food produce:-

- Air Drying by Hanging

- Mesh Air Drying

- Oven Drying

Oven Drying

Oven drying is an effective method but it also the least natural. It also requires you to check on the food regularly to ensure it is drying evenly and not burning.

Preheat your oven to the lowest setting. Use a baking sheet and spread out your plant, fruit or fungi evenly then pop it into the oven and leave it until it has fully dried.

Mesh Air Drying

Air drying is a natural and effective way to dry your foraged goods. Use a mesh screen which allows the air to circulate above, below and through it. Spread out your food on the top of your screen and place it in a cool, dry area. Make sure it has an inch or two beneath it to allow passage for the air.

You will need to turn your edibles from time to time to be certain that they dry evenly.

Air Drying by Hanging

Hanging your foraged items can add instant, old fashioned charm to your home and is a great way to dry your wild foods.

Gather the items together in small, loose bunches and tie them together by their stems. Do not place too many in each bunch as you will need the air to circulate around them to dry them properly.

As the moisture begins to release from the stems they will shrink slightly so an elastic band is the ideal thing to hold them together, but in the absence of an elastic band, tying them with string is fine.

Hang the tied bunches upside down and leave them to dry. Always dry your goods away from direct sunlight as the UV rays can cause the quality of the food to deteriorate.

Another way to hang dry is to use individual items or small bunches and peg them from a length of string or washing line.

When your produce is completely dried it should be quite brittle and crumble easily in your fingers. (Thicker food sources, such as fungi, can be sliced before drying if you prefer).

Crumble your dried food and store in an airtight container. Be sure to label each jar or container as you go because many items look the same or very similar one dried.

Chapter 4 – Foraged Food – Plants

Alexanders

Grows: All year round

Found: Fields, meadows, roadsides, woodland, this plant grows almost anywhere there is soil

Parts Used: Leaves, seeds

Taste & Smell: Extremely bitter tasting leaves and seeds, no distinctive smell.

Description:

Broad leaves, oval in shape and grow in a rosette. Some varieties have a leaf which is covered in fine white hairs. The flowers grow at the end of a long spike and very tiny. They grow in clusters and are yellow and/or white. Seeds are found at the top of the flower spikes.

Asparagus

Grows: April to June

Found: Gardens, waste ground, edges of woods, beside coastal roads

Parts Used: Asparagus Spears

Taste & Smell: Asparagus

Description:

Long, sparse, leaves with a feathery appearance but which are sharp to touch. The flowers are bell shaped and range from yellow to greenish white. They grow in clusters of 2 – 3 flowers and appear in the junction of the plants branches. The stem is woody and young plants produce triangular shaped leaf scales at its base.

Later in the year the plant produces red berries – these are Highly Toxic and should be avoided.

Basil

Grows: June to September

Found: Wild scrubland and dry, grassy areas

Parts Used: Leaves

Taste & Smell: Sweet, peppery taste and smell with a hint of mint

Description:

Leaves are ovate with slightly toothed edges and have little to no stem. Flowers are purple and white and appear in dense clusters at the top of a stem and grow between 1 and 2 cm long. The plant is not very tall and is slightly hairy.

Borage

Grows: March to October

Found: Anywhere there is soil

Parts Used: Flowers and young leaves

Taste & Smell: Cucumber

Description:

Mature leaves are oval in shape and hairy all over. Young leaves have few hairs. The leaves grow between 5 and 15 cm long. Stem of the plant is covered in coarse hairs. The flowers are primarily blue and have five triangular shaped petals which are quite narrow. Wild borage occasionally produces pink flowers.

Before the flowers appear the plant can be mistaken for Foxgloves or Green Alcanet so it is advisable to pick them only when they have flowered to avoid confusion.

Burdock

Grows: February to November

Found: Meadows, gardens, roadside, waste ground, edges of woodland and fields

Parts Used: Roots – Best harvested in spring or autumn. Stems, harvested between February and May.

Taste & Smell: Parsnips and sweet chestnuts. Leaves have a repugnant smell when crushed.

Description:

The leaves have dark green topsides with a lighter underside which is slightly hairy. Around the lower part of the plant the leaves are heart shaped but becoming narrower nearer to the flower stem. The stems start to become woody from the end of May onwards but, when young stems can be peeled and roasted. The plant has a tall stem which only appears when the plant has matured to over a year old. The roots are long and resemble black parsnips, but as the plant grows in stony ground they can be difficult to harvest. Flowers appear between midsummer and the autumn months and resemble purple thistle like flowers.

Chickweed

Grows: All year round

Found: Open woodland, fields, waste ground, parks, gardens, hedgerows

Parts Used: Young top leaves, lower leaves can be a little stringy

Taste & Smell: Lettuce

Description:

The leaves are small and pointed at the end with a round/oval shape. Generally chickweed leaves are smooth but sometimes present a slight covering of hair. The stems have a line of hairs down one side and are quite flimsy. Its flowers have five white petals which are split so they can often seem to be made up of ten petals.

Cleavers

Grows: Year round

Found: Paths and roadsides, hedgerows, woodland and waste ground

Parts Used: leaves, (at the top of plant) eaten cooked

Taste & Smell: Slightly bitter with a pea like scent

Description:

This is a little plant that has a slightly square shaped stem which is covered in tiny hooks. The leaves are small, thin and hairy and sprout in small rosettes. The flowers are very tiny and white. Seeds appear around summer time and are small, green and round. Ideally the leaves should be harvested before the seeds appear.

Coriander

Grows: Year round

Found: Hedges, roadsides, gardens, walls, riversides, fields, wasteland

Parts Used: Leaves, seeds, roots, flowers

Taste & Smell:

Description:

Coriander has slim, branched stems which grow up to 3 feet in height. It lower leaves are stemmed and have pinnate leaflets growing from the stem to form the whole leaf. The upper leaves are much slimmer with a larger divide. The flowers are pale purple and white and form in umbels. The seeds grow in cluster and appear first as green berries. As they ripen they will start to brown and drop from the plant.

Columbine

Grows; February to September

Found: Shaded meadows and woodlands. They are also commonly grown in gardens.

Parts Used: Flowers (all other parts of the plant are toxic)

Taste & Smell: Sweet

Description:

Columbine is a member of the buttercup family and have a long stem with 3 lobed leaves.

The flowers come in a variety of colors with the most common variations being purple and blue. They are made up of 5 small, rounded inner petals which surround the spurs at the centre. There are 5 larger outer petals which are longer and more tapered in shape.

It is advisable to discard the collection of the leaves as they require vigorous boiling to remove their toxicity. Seeds and roots of this plant are highly toxic in any form.

White Comfrey

Grows: May to October

Found: Riverside, marshland, damp woodland, damp grasses

Parts Used: Leaves

Taste & Smell: Hard to describe

Description:

Comfrey has clusters of bell shaped flowers that come in a variety of colors. ONLY white flowered comfrey leaves should be harvested. Before flowering this plant can be confused with Foxgloves.

Leaves are large and hairy with a broad base which tapers towards the end.

Common Sorrel

Grows: Year round

Found: Meadows, parks, fields, open woodland and lawns

Parts Used: Leaves

Taste & Smell: Sharp citrus taste with little smell

Description:

When young, this plant has short, rounded leaves with a shiny look to them. The base of a young sorrel leaf has a tiny tail which is pointed. As the plant matures the leaves become longer and arrow shaped. Mostly the leaves are green but red features can develop on them.

The plant develops a stem for the flowers which are long spikes of tiny yellow and red flowers.

Dead Nettles

Grows: Year round

Found: Woodland, roadsides, paths, parks

Parts Used: Leaves (cooked)

Taste & Smell: Tastes slightly like spinach and has a grass like smell

Description:

Leaves grow in pairs on opposite sides of the stem. They have a serrated edge and are covered in small hairs, (non-stinging). The stems are either red/purple or green and are covering in small non-stinging hairs. Flowers grow in small groups around the stem and are a variety of shades between white and yellow and red and purple.

Elder Tree

Grows: Year round

Found: Hedgerows, woodland, fields, parks,

Parts Used: Flowers and Berries

Taste & Smell: Flowers have a distinct sweet smell and have a mild, sweet taste. Elder flowers make a refreshing juice drink and excellent wines. Berries have little taste or smell but do compliment other flavors are best used in winemaking

Description:

The tree has a light colored bark with very brittle branches. Leave are toothed and closely resemble Ground Elder leave. Both leaves and bark are highly toxic.

Flowers are umbels of tiny white or cream flowers. The berries replace the flowers and are a small with a deep purple color.

Fat Hen

Grows: Year round

Found: Hedgerows, waste ground

Parts Used: Leaves, flowers and seeds

Taste & Smell: Cabbage

Description:

Leaves are a blue/green on the top with an occasional red flush. The underside has a silver sheen. They have slightly wavy edges that are toothed and are oval shaped. As they get higher up the plant they become more tapered and triangular in shape.

The flowers are spikes of tiny, white/green flowers that start at the base of the leaves.

Fennel

Grows: February to October

Found: roadsides, meadows, rocky hills and coastlines, woodland edges

Parts Used: Leaves and root, stems & flowers

Taste & Smell: Aniseed, sweet and fresh

Description:

Fennel has long stalks which grow closely together and can reach between 4 and 9 feet in height. They are topped with large clusters of yellow flowers. The leaves are long and feathery with widely spaced fronds. Its seeds are oblong shaped and ribbed.

The root is at the base of the leaves and is often quite large with a predominantly white and purple color. The distinctive smell of fennel stops it being confused with other plants.

Ground Elder

Grows: February to October

Found: Roadsides, in open fields, woodlands and gardens

Parts Used: Leaves

Smell & Taste: Slight spinach smell and taste

Description:

This plant grows almost anywhere and is commonly mistaken for a weed. It has toothed, ovate shaped leaves which grow in groups of thee with two additional leaves sometimes growing just below them. The leaves have a taste and smell very similar to sweet parsley.

The young leaves are a light green color and quite shiny. The young leaves add a nice taste to a salad.

Older leaves are a darker green and slightly dull. These can be cooked and are a good alternative to spinach.

From May to June, tight cluster of small, white flowers appear. Ground elder flowers have mild diuretic and laxative properties. Additionally they have soporific benefits so it is not advisable to eat the flowers. Their sleep inducing properties do not combine well with their diuretic and laxative properties.

Hairy Bittercress

Grows: Year round

Found: Pathways, light grass, bare soil, walls

Parts Used: Leaves

Taste & Smell: Slightly bitter and peppery with little smell

Description:

Leaves grow opposite each other in pairs along the entire leave stem with on final leaf at the end. It grows close to the ground and has flowering stems which ground a little above the leaf height. Flowers are tiny and white in color and grow in small groups.

Hawthorne

Grows: March to November

Found: Woodland, waste ground, hedgerows and is often planted in urban areas

Parts Used: Petals, leaves and berries

Taste & Smell: Flowers have a mild almond scent. The berries are sweet and have a slight apple taste to them. Leaves and petals add a nice touch to salads.

Description:

Leaves are dark green on the topside and slightly lighter colored underneath. They are deeply lobed. The flowers are small and white with five little petals.

Berries are stoned and vary from orange to deep red in color. They hang in cluster and present around the autumn months.

Hedge Garlic (Mustard Garlic)

Grows: March to September (Due to the plants biology it is able to survive through the winter months and can often be found even in the middle of winter)

Found: Shaded scrubland, woodlands and hedgerows

Parts Used: Seeds, flowers and leaves

Taste & Smell: Mixture of garlic and mustard

Description:

Hedge garlic has a two year cycle. Its first year produces small, broad heart shaped leaves which are close to the ground. In its second year the leaves become more triangular in shape and the leaf edges are serrated.

During its second year the stem grows upwards up to 130cm. Flowers grow in little clusters of small, white, four petal flowers with thin seeds pods.

The seeds, flowers and leaves are all edible and work great in both cooked foods and on salads.

Himalayan Balsam

Grows: March to November

Found: Close to riversides, ponds, streams lakes and in damp woodlands and meadows

Parts Used: Seeds, flowers and leaves

Taste & Smell: Leaves have no definable taste and can smell a little musty. Seeds have a nutty taste and work well in salads

Description:

This plant has red veined, green leaves with a red tinge on the serrated edges. The stem is hollow and smooth with a red hue. Flowers are hooded and come in a variety of shades of pink and purple. The seed pods appear from June to October.

Honesty

Grown: February to August

Found: Pathways, field edges, hedgerows, gardens and waste ground

Parts Used: Leaves, flowers, roots, seeds

Taste & Smell: Flowers and leaves have a slight cabbage taste with the flowers having a floral scent. Seeds and root taste like mustard

Description:

Leaves are oval with a pointed end and serrated edges. The flowers are purple or white and have a distinctive cross like shape and grow along the length of the tall stems.

The fruit of the plant contains the seeds and resembles silvery white pennies that are quite translucent.

Ladies Smock

Grows: March to August

Found: Fields, lawns, meadows, roadsides, river banks

Parts Used: leaves and flowers

Taste & Smell: Faint smell and tastes of sweet cress

Description:

Small, roundish leaves which grow in pairs opposite each other and end with a solitary leaf which grows close to the ground. The leaves become extremely thin closer to the stop of the stem, which is tall and thin.

The flowers are usually pale pink or pink but can occasionally present as white. They have 4 petals and grow at the top of the flower stem. Once the flowers die a very small, thin pod appears which contains the seeds.

Lesser Celendine

Grows: February to December

Found: Woodlands and gardens

Parts Used: Flowers, leaves and roots

Taste & Smell: No distinct smell. Leaves and flowers are slightly bitter. Roots MUST be cooked and have a sweet chestnut like taste.

Description:

This plant has fleshy, heart shaped leaves that have a noticeable shine. They are dark green in color. Flowers are similar to daisies but of a yellow color. The stem is quite short and predominantly green but can have a red or light brown hue.

The roots are shallow and knobbly and are a pale cream in color.

Mallow

Grown: Year round

Found: Roadsides, scrubland, hedgerows, waste ground, light woodland and alongside pathways

Parts Used: Young seed pods (often called cheeses) eaten raw or lightly steamed, young leaves eaten raw or deep fried

Taste & Smell: No discernible smell. Seed pods have a slight nutty flavor

Description:

Leaves are pentagon shaped and 5 lobed. They also have a tendency to be a little crinkled. Flowers are lilac colored and have a trumpet shape.

Mustard (Wild)

Grown: February to October

Found: Roadsides, field edges, waste ground, gardens, high sunny ground

Parts Used: Leaves, flowers and seeds

Taste & Smell: Sweet mustard

Description:

Leaves are hairy, lobed and have serrated edges. Lower leaves have their own stems, upper leave connect to the main plant stem. The stems are tall and quite strong and are often branched. Mainly green but can show purple coloring close to the leaves and branches.

Flowers are yellow and have four petals in a cross shape. They grow in clusters at the end of stem branches. Seeds are formed in pods following the flowering.

Nettle

Grown: year round

Found: Everywhere

Parts Used: Leaves (young leaves near the top of the plant only)

Taste & Smell: Nettles have a grass smell and taste a little like spinach after cooking

Description:

Green leaves with an arrow shaped form and serrated edges. The underside of the leaf is covered in small hairs which sting. Occasionally the topside of the leaf will have a few hairs. They grow opposite to each other in pairs, either side of the stem.

The male plant has green, yellow or purple flowers that are small and round. The females flowers have tiny little spike type petals emerging from the centre.

Pineapple Weed

Grown: May to September

Found: foot paths, field sides, waste ground and roadsides

Parts Used: Flower heads and leaves

Taste & Smell: Smells strongly of pineapple and tastes of sweet pineapple

Description:

Leaves grow in pairs opposite each other on either side of the stem. They have a spacious feathery look. The flowers are similar to daisies with white petals which quickly give way to the inner, dome shaped corollas which are yellow/green.

Ramsons – (Wild Garlic)

Grown: February to June

Found: Damp woodland area's often close to water

Parts Used: All parts

Taste & Smell: Strong Garlic

Description:

Ramsons has long, broad, single veined leaves, (narrower on young plants), and tiny groups of little white flowers which crown the stems. The stems taper towards the top and the whole plant has a strong garlic scent.

Although ramsons have a bulb shaped root, the flowers, seeds and leaves have a much nicer taste and are easier to collect, and by leaving the root intact the plant with re-grow.

Before flowering, the leaves resemble lily of the lily, (which is highly toxic), but the strong aroma of garlic makes it difficult to confuse.

Ribwort Plantain

Grown: march to November

Found: Meadows, fields, roadsides, parks, waste ground, woodland and sand dunes

Parts Used: Flower buds and stem

Taste & Smell: Very little smell but a mushroom-like taste. Leaves are very bitter so not great to eat.

Description:

The leaves are long, narrow and veined from base to tip. The stem belongs only to the flower, with the leaves growing directly from the ground. Flowers are very tiny and white and grow clustered together along the flower stalk.

Sheep' s Sorrel

Grown: Year round

Found: Fields, parks, open woodlands and parks

Parts Used: Leaves

Taste & Smell: Citrus smell with a mild apple taste

Description:

Sheep's sorrel has small, arrow shaped leaves which are lobed at the bottom. The leaves grow in rosettes and close to the ground. The stem is for the flower only. The flowers grow along the length of the flower stem and are tiny. Male plants have yellow/green petals and female's flowers are red.

Not a common plant so only pick what you need and only if there is a plentiful amount growing nearby.

Shepherds Purse

Grown: Year round

Found: Woodlands, waste ground, gardens

Parts Used: Young leaves and flower heads

Taste & Smell: Slightly peppery and cabbage like. No discernible smell

Description:

Leaves are varying and come in the form of either heavily toothed leaves or wavy leaves which grow in a rosette close to the ground. The stem is tall and thin and is topped with groups of tiny white flowers. The fruits from the flowers are green.

Sow Thistle

Grown: Year round

Found: Everywhere

Parts Used: Leaves and occasionally the roots

Taste & Smell: Leaves have a cabbage like taste

Description:

The base leaves grow in a rosette and are toothed. Further up the stem they become less toothed and produce a white sap when cut. The flowers closely resemble dandelions but one stem can produce many flowers. The roots are quite small but can be roasted.

Stagshorn Plantain

Grown: Year round

Found: Fields, lawns, pavements, waste ground, meadows, coastlines and anywhere there is gravelly or sandy soil

Parts Used: Leaves

Taste & Smell: Leaves have no discernible smell but taste like a nutty parsley

Description:

Leaves are quite distinctive and resemble the antlers on a deer. Younger leaves are less defined. All are often coated with a layer of fine hairs. They grow in a rosette close to the grown with the stem belonging only to the flowers. The flowers are quite large and cylindrical with a light brownish color.

Wood Avens

Grown: Year round

Found: Shaded areas, woodlands and hedgerows

Parts Used: Leaves and root

Taste & Smell: Leaves have little to no smell or taste. The roots smell and taste of cloves. Young leaves can be deep fried

Description:

Leaves grow in a rosette close to the ground. They have three lobes covered with light downy hairs. The stem appears to facilitate flowering and leaves spread up along the stem, growing in pairs opposite each other, becoming smaller as they reach the top.

The flowers have five petals that are small and bright yellow in colour. The roots are plentiful and strong.

Yarrow - Edible

Grown: March to November

Found: Fields, beside roads and meadows

Parts Used: Leaves

Taste & Smell: Antiseptic scent with a mild antiseptic taste

Description:

Long, slim, feathery like leaves with clusters of small pink or white flowers. (The flowers appear from June to September).

Yarrow has a strong medicinal smell and is mainly used in medicines but the leaves can be a nice addition to a salad.

Chapter 5 – Foraged Food – Flowers

Apple Blossom

Apple blossoms can enhance the look of any meal and taste great. They have a gentle, slightly floral taste and go well with salads and desserts. Try a few blossoms on the side of an apple pie with cream or sprinkle some flowers into a cold glass of lemonade. Delicious but eat with caution. Only consume 2 or 3 flowers at most at any time. Too many can leave you with an upset stomach.

Carnations

The more fragrant the carnation, the more pronounced the taste. The majority of Dianthus species have a floral, clove like flavor with a hint of spice. They are great for garnishing salads and soups and work well with sorbets, fruit salads and ice-cream. Only eat the petals though as the base of the flower has quite a bitter taste.

Cornflowers

These beautiful flowers can be used to add a touch of summer to omelettes, pasta dishes and salads. They mix well with other flowers and come in a variety of colors. The strength of flavor can differ slightly from flower to flower but range from a sweet to a spicy clove flavor.

Geranium

Geranium leaves have a strong citrus flavor and work well mixed into cake mixes, cheesecakes and many other deserts. The flowers also have a citrus flavor but it is more subtle and works well as a garnish.

Lavender

Whether you are making sweet or savory dishes, jams or sauces, lavender can compliment them all. Lavender sugar is delicious with its sweet but subtle flavor. Try drizzling some over pancakes.

Lilac

Lilacs have a strong fragrance and a light, lemony flavor. Although they work well with any salad, their citrusy taste can add a whole new dimension to fresh cream, cream cheeses and plain yoghurts. Mix them into any of these and your food will take on a lovely, fresh tang.

Nasturtiums

Nasturtium leaves and flowers have a similar taste to the peppery watercress. Eaten on their own as a garnish or on a salad they add a spicy element to your food. They can also be finely chopped and mixed into cream cheese or butter to add a kick to your lunchtime sandwich.

Pansy

Pansies have a mild lettuce type flavor but they are quite plain. They are best used as a garnish and can make any meal look inviting with a few flowers and petals spread over it. They lend themselves well to decorating desserts, cheeseboards and salads.

Rose

Roses have a gentle flavor which enhances fruit desserts or juices. Both the rosehip and the petals add a delicate flavor to jams, jellies and even relishes. They also add a splash of color and drama to a plain salad or soup dish. All colors of rose can be used with subtle differences in flavor depending on the strain of rose you pick. The more fragrant the rose, the stronger the flavor will be.

Sunflower

Most people look to sunflowers for their seeds, but the petals are edible too. The petals have a mild nutty flavor which works well with salads and yoghurt based dips.

Chapter 6 – Foraged Food – Berries

Blackberries

Grows: March to October

Found: Waste land, woodland, hedgerows, in fact, most places that are not regularly well maintained.

Description:

Leaves on blackberry bushes can vary from palm to oval shapes. The stems are strong an thorny and the plants regularly produce an abundance of delicious fruit which can be made in desserts, used in salads, turned in jams or used to make delicious drinks and wines. The small flowers have 5 white or pale pink petals and grow in clusters prior to the fruit developing. The spring leaves make a delicious addition to a fresh salad.

Blackthorn (Sloe) Tree

Grows: September to December

Found: Woodland and field edges

Description:

The blackthorn tree/bush has a dark colored bark and is full of thorns was exercise caution when collecting the fruits. The leaves are serrated and oval shaped. Flowers are made up of 5 petals which are a creamy white color and form prior to the berries.

The berries are a best cooked or used for making gin or wine. Eaten raw they can make your mouth extremely dry.

Damson Tree

Fruit Grows: September to October

Found: Woodlands, alongside pavements, in parks and hedgerows

Description:

The damson tree is a small to medium height tree and has oval leaves with a serrated edge. The leaves are shiny and a dark green in color. Flowers form with five petals and in small clusters before the fruit develops. Fruits are small, oval and of a very dark blue/black color. They are sweet tasting and resemble a small plum.

Wild Raspberry

Grows: July to September

Found: Woodland, woodland clearings, roadsides

Description:

The fruit of a wild raspberry plant usually makes an appearance between summer and autumn. The leaves have five or seven serrated leaflets and a quite thin. Flowers have five petals and precede the fruit.

Chapter 7 – Foraged Food – 10 Common Fungi

Beefsteak Fungus

Grows: August to November

Found: Grows on living or dead chestnut or oak trees

Size: maximum width – 20 cm

Description:

Creamy white pores cover the underside of the cap which will bruise to a red/brown color is damaged. The stem is rarely seen but when it is it will be short and thick. The cap is semi-circular and looks like a tongue. When young the edges are slightly inflated but this flattens as it matures. The cap is either red or a variation of red/pink/brown. It is also usually a little sticky or moist to touch. The inner flesh is red with white veins which resemble meat.

Cauliflower Fungus

Grows: September to November

Found: On the roots of pine and other conifers. Can sometimes be found around the base of the trunk

Size: Maximum height – 25 cm Maximum width – 25 cm

Description:

This mushroom has a slight rooting stem which will be mostly underground. The caps resemble a sea sponge or a brain and are made up of flattened lobes that range from yellowy grey to light brown to creamy white in color. The inner flesh is off white in the centre but darkens towards the edges.

Dryads Saddle

Grows: February to August

Found: Deciduous trees and trunks

Size: Maximum – 60 cm

Description:

The stem is quite woody and can grow up to 8 cm tall and often darkens to black at the base. The underside of the cap has large, angular, off white colored pores that are irregular in pattern. The cap is a large fan shape or circular which is yellow to ochre colored. It has darker circles of brown scales. The inner flesh is succulent and thick when young but becomes leathery with age.

Field Blewit

Grows: Year round

Found: meadows and grasslands, often grows in groups

Size: Maximum width – 12 cm

Description:

The stem of these is off white and has a blue/lilac covering. It is short, chunky and swollen at the base. Cap underside is white to off white and busy. The cap is convex and of a beige to grey brown color with a white inner flesh.

Giant Puffball

Grows: July to November

Found: Woodside edges, field and meadow edges, roadsides and open woodland

Size: Maximum width – from 10 cm up to 80 cm (yes, really)

Description:

These massive fungi are quite rare in the UK and Ireland but they do appear from time to time. This is a large, almost spherical shaped ball of fungi which is impossible to mistake for anything else. There is no stem, no mid section, just a huge ball filled with fungi spores and flesh. The underside, (when you can see it), starts off white and turns to yellow then brown as it ages. It is filled with spores so help yourself to as much as you like if you are lucky enough to find one, but tear a little off and spread it around so more will grow.

Hedgehog Fungus

Grows: August to November

Found: Woodland

Size: Maximum height – 8 cm Maximum width – 18 cm

Description:

The gills and stem of this fungus is covered in spines which can grow up to 6 mm long and vary in color from white to salmon pink. The stem is often off centre where it meets the caps. The cap is convex and uneven and occasionally has depressions around the centre. It is a creamy yellow color or pale flesh/salmon colored.

Oyster Mushroom

Grows: Year round

Found: Grows in large, shelf like groups on the trunks, stumps or fallen branches of deciduous trees

Size: Maximum width – 15 cm

Description:

These fungi stems are often difficult to find as the caps appear to grow directly from the tree. The stems are white and open out into the cap which is shaped similar to a clam when young. This flattens as the Fungi gets larger. The caps vary in color from grey, smoky grey, silver and brown. Other varieties of oyster mushrooms are pink, white or yellow but all are edible. CAUTION: There is one mushroom that is very similar to an oyster mushroom but is poisonous. To be certain you are collecting edible oysters, check over the group they are growing in. So long as at least one mushroom cap is the size of the palm of a hand, they are safe. The poisonous look alike does not grow any larger than the size of a 2 pence piece.

Penny Bun

Grows: August to November

Found: Woodlands

Size: Maximum Height – 25 cm Maximum Width – 20 cm

Description:

The underside of the penny bun fungi has pores and a white spongy flesh which yellows with age. It has a thick, bulbous stem with a fine mesh-like covering just underneath the cap. It has white flesh when young which yellows as it ages. The cap is quite bulbous in its infancy but flattens slightly as it grows. When fully matured the cap resembles a crusty brown bread roll. It is great to eat either raw or cooked. This fungus strengthens in smell and flavor when dried.

Scarlet Elf Cup

Grows: January to April

Found: In clusters on dead wood

Size: Maximum Height – 3 cm Maximum Width – 6 cm

Description:

These fungi have very short stems which are covered with fine hairs. The underside of the cup has small pores and is also covered with fine hair. The cup is a bright scarlet color with a defined cupped shape. As the fungi matures the cups begins to flatten into a shallower disk. The underside is a much paler color than the top. It has a very mild mushroom taste.

Wood Ears

Grows: Year round

Found: On Elder Trees

Size: Maximum 12 cm width

Description:

These are not the most attractive or flavorsome of fungi but you can be sure that if you collect them of an elder tree only, you are picking the right thing.

They are a tan or red/brown color and have a slightly jellylike feel and look a little like ears. The underside is often a little paler in color and smoother to touch than the top. They must be cooked well before eating and work well as a base for stock.

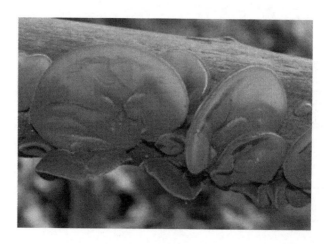

Conclusion

Thank you again for buying this book!

I hope this book was able to help you to recognize how much fun it can be to forage for your own food and has given you a good base with which to start.

The next step is to grab your family and friends, get into your wellingtons and waterproofs and head outside to see what you can find.

I wish you lots of luck and laughter on your foraging adventures

Finally, if you enjoyed this book, then I'd like to ask you for a favor, would you be kind enough to leave a review for this book on Amazon? It'd be greatly appreciated!

Thank you and good luck!

Manufactured by Amazon.ca
Bolton, ON

26444781R00044